The Helpful WEEKLY PLANNER and To-Do List for PRODUCTIVE DOERS

I0187416

Activinotes

Activinotes

DAILY JOURNALS, PLANNERS, NOTEBOOKS AND OTHER BLANK BOOKS

Weekly Planner

MONDAY	TUESDAY	WEDNESDAY	To Do List

THURSDAY	FRIDAY	SATURDAY	To Buy List

SUNDAY		To Do List

Weekly Planner

Weekly Planner

Weekly Planner

MONDAY	TUESDAY	WEDNESDAY	To Do List

THURSDAY	FRIDAY	SATURDAY	To Buy List

SUNDAY			To Do List

Weekly Planner

Weekly Planner

Weekly Planner

MONDAY	TUESDAY	WEDNESDAY	To Do List

THURSDAY	FRIDAY	SATURDAY	To Buy List

SUNDAY			To Do List

Weekly Planner

Weekly Planner

Weekly Planner

MONDAY	TUESDAY	WEDNESDAY	To Do List

THURSDAY	FRIDAY	SATURDAY	To Buy List

SUNDAY			To Do List

Weekly Planner

Weekly Planner

Weekly Planner

MONDAY	TUESDAY	WEDNESDAY	To Do List

THURSDAY	FRIDAY	SATURDAY	To Buy List

SUNDAY			To Do List

Weekly Planner

Weekly Planner

Weekly Planner

MONDAY	TUESDAY	WEDNESDAY	To Do List

THURSDAY	FRIDAY	SATURDAY	To Buy List

SUNDAY		To Do List

Weekly Planner

Weekly Planner

Weekly Planner

MONDAY	TUESDAY	WEDNESDAY	To Do List

THURSDAY	FRIDAY	SATURDAY	To Buy List

SUNDAY	To Do List

Weekly Planner

Weekly Planner

Weekly Planner

MONDAY	TUESDAY	WEDNESDAY	To Do List

THURSDAY	FRIDAY	SATURDAY	To Buy List

SUNDAY	To Do List

Weekly Planner

Weekly Planner

Weekly Planner

MONDAY	TUESDAY	WEDNESDAY	To Do List

THURSDAY	FRIDAY	SATURDAY	To Buy List

SUNDAY		To Do List

Weekly Planner

Weekly Planner

Weekly Planner

MONDAY	TUESDAY	WEDNESDAY	To Do List

THURSDAY	FRIDAY	SATURDAY	To Buy List

SUNDAY	To Do List

Weekly Planner

Weekly Planner

Weekly Planner

MONDAY	TUESDAY	WEDNESDAY	To Do List

THURSDAY	FRIDAY	SATURDAY	To Buy List

SUNDAY	To Do List

Weekly Planner

Weekly Planner

Weekly Planner

MONDAY	TUESDAY	WEDNESDAY	To Do List

THURSDAY	FRIDAY	SATURDAY	To Buy List

SUNDAY		To Do List

Weekly Planner

Weekly Planner

Weekly Planner

MONDAY	TUESDAY	WEDNESDAY	To Do List

THURSDAY	FRIDAY	SATURDAY	To Buy List

SUNDAY	To Do List

Weekly Planner

Weekly Planner

Weekly Planner

MONDAY	TUESDAY	WEDNESDAY	To Do List

THURSDAY	FRIDAY	SATURDAY	To Buy List

SUNDAY	To Do List

Weekly Planner

Weekly Planner

Weekly Planner

MONDAY	TUESDAY	WEDNESDAY	To Do List

THURSDAY	FRIDAY	SATURDAY	To Buy List

SUNDAY			To Do List

Weekly Planner

Weekly Planner

Weekly Planner

MONDAY	TUESDAY	WEDNESDAY	To Do List

THURSDAY	FRIDAY	SATURDAY	To Buy List

SUNDAY	To Do List

Weekly Planner

Weekly Planner

Weekly Planner

MONDAY	TUESDAY	WEDNESDAY	To Do List

THURSDAY	FRIDAY	SATURDAY	To Buy List

SUNDAY			To Do List

Weekly Planner

Weekly Planner

Weekly Planner

MONDAY	TUESDAY	WEDNESDAY	To Do List

THURSDAY	FRIDAY	SATURDAY	To Buy List

SUNDAY			To Do List

Weekly Planner

Weekly Planner

Weekly Planner

MONDAY	TUESDAY	WEDNESDAY	To Do List

THURSDAY	FRIDAY	SATURDAY	To Buy List

SUNDAY	To Do List

Weekly Planner

Weekly Planner

Weekly Planner

MONDAY	TUESDAY	WEDNESDAY	To Do List

THURSDAY	FRIDAY	SATURDAY	To Buy List

SUNDAY		To Do List

Weekly Planner

Weekly Planner

Weekly Planner

MONDAY	TUESDAY	WEDNESDAY	To Do List

THURSDAY	FRIDAY	SATURDAY	To Buy List

SUNDAY		To Do List

Weekly Planner

Weekly Planner

Weekly Planner

MONDAY	TUESDAY	WEDNESDAY	To Do List

THURSDAY	FRIDAY	SATURDAY	To Buy List

SUNDAY		To Do List

Weekly Planner

Weekly Planner

Weekly Planner

MONDAY	TUESDAY	WEDNESDAY	To Do List

THURSDAY	FRIDAY	SATURDAY	To Buy List

SUNDAY			To Do List

Weekly Planner

Weekly Planner

Weekly Planner

MONDAY	TUESDAY	WEDNESDAY	To Do List

THURSDAY	FRIDAY	SATURDAY	To Buy List

SUNDAY	To Do List

Weekly Planner

Weekly Planner

Weekly Planner

MONDAY	TUESDAY	WEDNESDAY	To Do List

THURSDAY	FRIDAY	SATURDAY	To Buy List

SUNDAY		To Do List

Weekly Planner

Weekly Planner

Weekly Planner

MONDAY	TUESDAY	WEDNESDAY	To Do List

THURSDAY	FRIDAY	SATURDAY	To Buy List

SUNDAY			To Do List

Weekly Planner

Weekly Planner

Weekly Planner

MONDAY	TUESDAY	WEDNESDAY	To Do List

THURSDAY	FRIDAY	SATURDAY	To Buy List

SUNDAY	To Do List

Weekly Planner

Weekly Planner

Weekly Planner

MONDAY	TUESDAY	WEDNESDAY	To Do List

THURSDAY	FRIDAY	SATURDAY	To Buy List

SUNDAY		To Do List

Weekly Planner

Weekly Planner

Weekly Planner

MONDAY	TUESDAY	WEDNESDAY	To Do List

THURSDAY	FRIDAY	SATURDAY	To Buy List

SUNDAY		To Do List

Weekly Planner

Weekly Planner

Weekly Planner

MONDAY	TUESDAY	WEDNESDAY	To Do List

THURSDAY	FRIDAY	SATURDAY	To Buy List

SUNDAY		To Do List

Weekly Planner

Weekly Planner

Weekly Planner

MONDAY	TUESDAY	WEDNESDAY	To Do List

THURSDAY	FRIDAY	SATURDAY	To Buy List

SUNDAY			To Do List

Weekly Planner

Weekly Planner

Weekly Planner

MONDAY	TUESDAY	WEDNESDAY	To Do List

THURSDAY	FRIDAY	SATURDAY	To Buy List

SUNDAY	To Do List

Weekly Planner

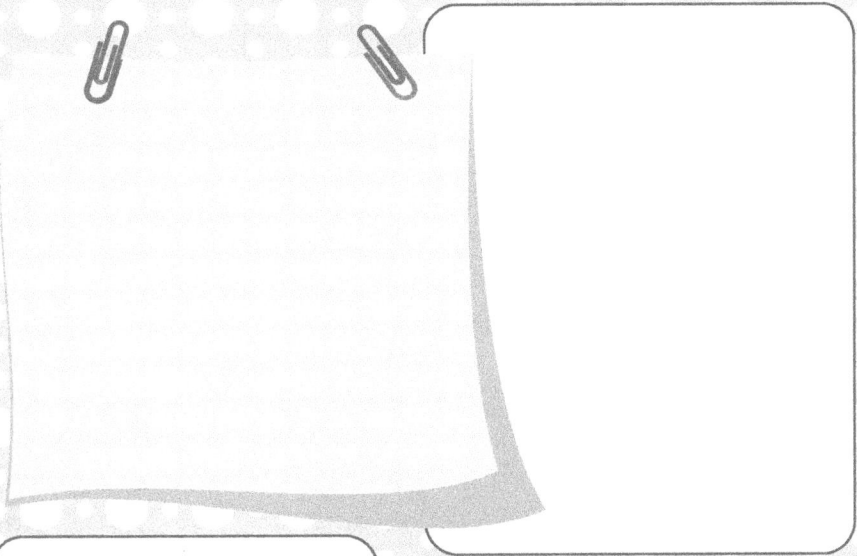

Weekly Planner

Weekly Planner

MONDAY	TUESDAY	WEDNESDAY	To Do List

THURSDAY	FRIDAY	SATURDAY	To Buy List

SUNDAY			To Do List

Weekly Planner

Weekly Planner

Weekly Planner

MONDAY	TUESDAY	WEDNESDAY	To Do List

THURSDAY	FRIDAY	SATURDAY	To Buy List

SUNDAY			To Do List

Weekly Planner

Weekly Planner

Notes

www.ingramcontent.com/pod-product-compliance
Lightning Source LLC
Chambersburg PA
CBHW081337090426
42737CB00017B/3182